RIMMING THE EVENT HORIZON

Sabeen Chaudhry

Published 2023 by the87press
The 87 Press LTD
87 Stonecot Hill
Sutton
Surrey
SM3 9HJ
www.the87press.co.uk

ISBN: 978-1-7393939-4-6

Printed and bound by CPI Group (UK) Ltd, Croydon, CR0 4YY

Artwork by Sabeen Chaudhry & Chris Warsop
Design: Stanislava Stoilova [www.sdesign.graphics]

For my parents

I've kept one foot in the universe
that's why I am so incomplete
I've licked death with my tongue
therefore I taste bitter.

—Sara Shagufta

♦

She's tasting her own tears and she is weightless and deadly.
—Dionne Brand

♦

At the center [sic] of the cyclone everything cracks, everything
collapses in the ripping sound of great manifestations.
—Suzanne Césaire

♦

Because only the end of the world as we know it, I am
convinced, can dissolve cultural differences' production of
human collectives as 'strangers.'
—Denise Ferreira da Silva

SPECK VIOLENCE

run

reeling in the badlands of our glottal roaming
small stars are floored, instituting
a loquacious reign of longing & destruction
saying things, we freewheel, cartwheel through craters
stroke my spine and I'll poison you, rub my belly and I'll giggle
at high volumes, high altitudes, items stream from our mouths
hurl themselves off cliffs as below
eyes widen under waves
surfaces are woken by survival
we like nothing we say but accept all these
oracular horrors as things
that make themselves as us, switching sides
      we're dismayed to find that we don't drown easily
      snails on the bed blinking slowly as we sink

bust

gluttony is cramming the spectre
with expectation, flaunting
20,000 luxuries under the sea
unliking the sound of treasure
fresh refract, *tinnitus empire!* trickle-
down-swung molten neither
terraperforming charity nor lending
deep-fake grace in crenelated gloom
when our ground blossoms down there
sudden & with secret attitude
they seize, bloom-entitled hydrotate
but we moisturise, then trip the sneeze
       boom weirder than the repercussions
       outsmarting even pulchritude

nyctinasty

can't be innocent in the night
wingspan of a *fatwa*, relaying
gossip that stings our eyes

making a fist with love, closing
with the silence of cellulose
holding the texture of darkness

> *the fingernail dreams of scratching*
> *the itch in state lacquer*

on the underside of beauty we
wriggle in the earth
triumphant w/o faces

jasmine scents in roiling segments
wavelength of swagger proportional to suffering
kindness   running faster   in the dark

> *there are things that jump*
> *and things that fall*

lather

it's a leggy day in spring
when all seconds of the
sprout predict pink. after
lunch, i wash the city's
mouth out with soap and
dump my crusts in the
Ladies' Pond. lagging in
the leaking that deafens
all dimensions; teleology
blinks broke on amber at
the lights. i duck the spills
and jaywalk. in trodden-
on blossoms as temporary
tattoos, we write 'expensive
spores' on a post-it and
stick it on the damp party
wall. outside, the city
kicks dolour out of its
nest and powder blue eggs
smash on the pavement.

make her rob a motherfucking bank

abysmal fawn pyroclastic *I*

pretty cry through The Revolution

looking like a victimless crime

all trending excruciations   petty thefts

hot swimming the halocline

small_fire_soak

abyssal in my salinity

anoxic for perfect lines

between damp infamies

if it fits

wade across with your big and slender
feet wide flit of the tenured eternal &
reversible hair flick special slide I hated
him getting lost at sea
all cry-faced & inevitable email
not enough smokes and sweets
a lost shoe, pleiotropic return to drink
didn't deserve me anyway
cheer up simply your space
again evicted, a British Asian smile
there is no original step
so plink predictable v v crassly
prêt-à-porter & hot-to-trot

false

gash love in the rut
with the swelter of
my face, a wrong symbol
in the omniphobic gush
contra meatless falsetto
sometimes so hard to know
whether to sigh or sign off
that deadname we've been
calling Dignity

    a makeshift *pissoir*

      brashly tells her to die in Pakistan

direct-to-consume all *faux pas*

      I vote for the significant warmth of your hands

        crusade to triple-lock   aging itself

        gallant as the grander scheme
        and   galling   the   nook
        of   your   life

eutrophication

it's an algal day in summer
when all seconds of the wind
remain green. your birthday
breezes in overbloom w/
personages of sun. we're
burning in the bossing and
hiding in the courgette
flowers of the rich. (photonic
flourish of VIPs.) the city
celebrates salting the wound
with a cream cake from
Finchley and karaoke-like
heat stroke, looking deep
into your eyes and dedicating
the song to you which causes
you to faint. we can only be
here as intermediaries, you
know? friends of friends at
best. we eat in the street and
despite knowing better,
swoon in the auspicious hour
of the most vicious animal.

shopping

mine is an impossible blue
product gone, asymptomatic scattering
of snow, confetti, last chance
entelechy as quiet quitting
glib as an empty shelf
settled by dust in rotation
between stillness and its opposite
there is something else
thumps like enough
tephra to coat the world
in a new look for a nuclear winter
asymptotic cuffing or next best
case scenario: the whole the (w)hole
the ()hole demure, evaporating or never
quite getting close enough
it's true that
she was always cold

cull

in the ached furl of our girlhood

the hot-cold of motherly subsidence

       diachronous as silt & slide

       ride_or_die

every suburban street: an opportunity

for precocity, a sed(im)entary smirk

basking post-megafauna

in colonial overkill, resting

on their laurels   milk it

milk it till it's blind

angle

no one tells me if I'm here or gone
glowering in one of many aftermaths

in one world they all drowned, in another
suffocated in the lorried lore of the land

elsewhere the *good people* pretend to care
congratulate themselves with branding

gaslit desire strikes the match for removal
swift as any credible spark

ground that lift-off spite with the grabbed
& loving azimuth of a different 2nd gen orbital

that old scream in ink revealed
with the lifted trouser leg

someone else's memory of one swan
on a pond at Calais, a limp, no doctor

guess none of us really know what to say
but we know we want to say it

sleeping on the floor all over Europe, the kids
swivel grief a talent & will speak the mystery of arrival

silvagenitus

it's a foliar day in autumn when
all seconds of the sky sip yellow.
a different city formally asks
you to move your scar. soot and
the tail end of a glass noodle
slipping a note up your nostril. in
the woods on the hill we try
waifing to each other through the
wisp light, while the city rolls us
lonely round a tree with your name
carved in. the past lives of other
cities congregate here sometimes,
creaking, smoking, croaking
us a long goodbye but cheaper.
still we don't drive, hug without
warning and the Christmas tree
festers in the garage for a year.

returns

fake_laughing
flash the circle in dust
decorous & blow
death in their eyes

get them back w/
shallow lurk cavitation
                  sundew ready
                  ageless &
                  clever as the moment

uncoil

when I was moulting their bodies
as a charming puzzle of England, I was hissing
in the air kiss, disarming all the partygoers
flirting, wronged & buttered
melting all careers—*cheers!*
bitter & bursting the dawn
of our aptitudes—*darlings!*
the seam of our dysrepair

a button flies off into space
to orbit their politics
cheeky satellite: watching, careening
& waiting to crash

stain removal

I hunt the cloud for hours
then with a tapered look
harpoon it right out of the sky:
great white stain, slapped
swimming pink cheeks
dysmember blushed lossy
fake crying
into my hair

signs

it's a locked day in winter when all
seconds of the spikes taunt scarlet.
brushing past bushes in puffas, we let
ducks go ahead at the canalside. shortcut
our souls to situated murk. i overheard
bubbles = life. the city subsists on rust,
blood fled and dead berries. it gets a tooth
pulled and goes to the food bank for the
first time. 'two hundred more parks than
Paris,' it repeats while a handful of rusty
nails scatter in its wake. we give it some
chocolate. at home, we light candles,
crack our joints and cough. the city
opens a tin of tomato soup and short-
circuits our hearts for the onslaught.

my heart's not true

infra_swirling

      in new inflations of wet microburst

        taxonomic soil technics sifting fatal

I want to be perma_

frost_footed and free

     released from strategy

       and caring too much

   unextracted, a wince

from an icy heel on a hot thigh

orographic

interning the dawn, dunked
skewered metric
of inclining

skip
droop & dredge
through these
dyslocal streets, red
in my hair brings mountain
sassed as stone, so-
called 'dirty mind'
as subterranean
encumbrance
skyward
yawn

inqilab, my shadow
to throw, melismatic my
heat dome   my amulet   my pebble   my spinning
continually constituted
as a curse

saviour

forgetting the silver squiggle
earning through sky, roiling
in the subsidised circumference we
swat the radius pirouetting
to check our bank accounts & clap
lack on the back, push it out the door
never surrender spelling out
today, umbilical, blank in the middle
pass out & pay, densely divorced
from every sad thing, living in the exit
(gift) bag at the end of all feeling
....
a pothole a pitfall a dragon
and a woman make a pact

In more ways than one, I didn't choose to be here, screaming through the flag.

A car passes behind me and makes the sound the angel of death makes.

There's always one thick Asian in every White supremacist group.

It's funny how they commit suicide to escape love and we do it to escape them.

Yes! We will burn down heaven and flood the fires of hell!

OUR WHORLS

Tail

Hello old lady
riding ultramafic on the backs of tigers
jigarkhor-type, a spine
of solid supernova & seducing.
Show me how to make eyes at the boys:
eroto-hepatic extractions for laughs
w/ the daughters of the valley plaiting before &
after, thick as ravens smogging the sky with escape.
'Did you see his face unzipped? No need for *lathis*,'
liverless lads bleeding lust all over the sheep
-ish contingent husband crowing the value
of disaster & flight.

The Moment smashes a fan's phone on stage
as I oil the vectors of *émigré* flummox
on the pilgrimage of speculative lustre, sly
and unattainable syntropic plumage
as if synchrony could ever be our beauty standard
                                        old lady.
She says, 'all I can offer you is heat death, nuance & terror,'
and I say, 'I'll take it!' (Again, like I always do
a soft touch when she swings the rope.)

And yet in the hall of mirrors & down, of fluff & fucks
she is the warm hand of undercurrent unhinged from sequence
the calloused nevermind of my passing through
airports and apartments, rice fields & atmospheres
(though she refuses to jump out of a cake or a box).
Her line appears and dysappears on my palm
a crack of black pepper the thunder the fault
line the choke. 'Hold on,' she commands and I dysfigure.

Cryptophasic counting backwards I hide
and she seeks faster than solar surf
unmothering herself with gerontic glee.
How can it be this hard to stay still? She knows
we can never have peace and yet wants me
to breach the wave with my breath
while she puts this moment   here
                                    & here
a gasp and I'm beached in no time.

I can't pretend I don't cherish the forgery
of her presence: there is only the one jig
and we do it well. Fireworks over the wall
without the ticket, under the water
a fairground on fire with no wherewithal
never recovering from anything and I am jogging
her memory on loop with the voice that we hate
saying, 'what next?'

Hear the Thames groan in the night
unwaged and not sleeping, our shifty
new boy needing gastric lavage
tossing & turning a trigeminal dash—
the shit the water the cholera the eels the sludge
magic the weapons the teeth and weird plastic
a balloon and the bottled messages subtracting.
And now   *old lady*
dressed as a rocket on Waterloo Bridge
ungoth me trending with the cost of wings.

again

                that same kind of piracy as in a kiss / commuting
in the tube carriage we're cartoon livestock
                        immurement
           jewel & sugar death
blossomèd in the wallèd garden
(she was everybody's favourite)   (fruit w/o guile)
are you scared of a dot
              LARPing as your life?
              selling indigo from Bayana in 1608
caesura at the party in pavement syncopal
    'Could I behold the face of my beloved once more–'
to think your waist still / twisting
                    as you throw the rock
is soft-porn neotectonica, smoking
    flicking ash into the LA basin
                       off the crystalline rim
      preferring your selfies to be taken
              from a higher dimension
so hyperbolically spaced / migrated
        curls correlating, unbrush
our hair in unison   apart
ending so hard for those latent topologies
                  (to have & to hold)
    'I would thank God until the day of resurrection.'
winking at each other in the one wave / all-
         (she's not going to put it online)
matched-out-at-a-distance   indentured
      to this weak quantum biting
          the universe really *works* at loving itself
(you're the chef in my dream it's my birthday)
                telltale photon where I've been

blushing nonlocality in sob-trance-particulate
violence of the possibilistic lick
administered tumbling from the tearful mouth of difference
rejecting the mattered vacuum w/ tender precision
addicts of
the ripple
new gold dangle
attics & staircases
flanked disturbance
(just want to sit next to you while you drive)
swing your heaven/hell legs
sitting on the wall L/R

fire   & re-hire   myself

into iterative redundancy

as   never   as   this

G.

This season I wear
my begrudging resilience in orange
aglow in the belly of my vanishing
deferred   at every moment
a rediscovered flower
named after its own extinction

though I am no Lazarus no miracle
clear-cutting for your recursive guilt
& minus stain understory.

I have been here all along, taking cover under wisped solidarity
in dew-pointed defiance while you were all so very sure I was
dead. When I pass over the edge of the ridge, I will appear to
you as an apparition while simultaneously reincarnating in an
unknown location. All-Boy All-Girl, I could be   sea glass
                             peaches
                           jealousy.
When the White man comes to take a sample, I am hacked by
his racialising whimsy. *That haggering erotics of the specimen!*

        There is limerence & yolk
           in the sound of trees being felled.

Enter disloyalty of a haggling mist.

I hush myself post-dryadic

                    (post-woman)
                    (post-evil)

processual lesser   goddess.

Come-and-go now they, all soil & somersault in blood of the sap kind, propagate themselves in this dysgrow and disgust me. They can only say what runs green and/or red, doesn't matter as us in the way they think, though we turned blaze our forte anyway: Flickering sprouts fogged for safety and all split-up but calling kin and beyond in a language of whispering beacons.

Oh, you love me now, do you?

            diligent herb
surprising petal
            bruised verticality
chic cutting
            phylled with   survivor epiphany

Assimilating into my own end(s)!

(Centinela finale on repeat.)

But surely you didn't think I'd go that easily! Rolling my
'r's and falling my name. He looks into my eyes in stupid
physiognomic spree, grunting and I bite him. I will bite him
until every end and then after, until the next one and again.
Flail cyclical in not-steam amid my jaw & my decisions. One
of me will rub his face in it, while others go off to undulate or
glimmer, drip, delight or covet.

Necrobiome

This universe eats

 all the feelings I won't have

 my questions about the neutrality of snow

 my father (*no really*)

  all drastic wrong glossing

  the pace of my walk-away.

I am quietly confident, seeped

    and scattered, tacitly histrionic

 as starshine launders my dreams to deify

  the unsafety of scavenger nicetimes

   nematodic decadence defying outside

/ inside as thanatomicrobial baroque

  begging to bloat the post-mortem sociality

of our revolving 'invasions', trying

 to stratopause racialisation's staring

   loop-the-loops between heavens and dirt

              displaced soil on the soles

      and souls of our names, wallowing

         in a plenitude decomposed for twinkle

and scraping a living so flinched in *un*

    -doing what we do like looks could kill

            sequestered in crumbs plucked

    wily with the timbre of a cliff-hanger.

Compacted with contrapuntal grief

    weaponise our love as divine pestilence

        the fugue or the plague comes as daggers

     to the heart or flecks of mud

         clear as revenge shrugged on the tips

    of our tongues, lethal snowflake, *you cannot*

      die if you never lived!

but still our kids die of mould inhalation

to a soundtrack of politicians' crocodile tears

and handshakes that make it rain   and snow

and snow without the heating on.

I sniff-out future clandestine graves, truly

you can't slip one past me in this

elegant epinecrotics of dyslocated *we*

astral project into a coffee cup or tea leaves

and I will show you where to find the body

the bodies swishing my thoughts to tick

the microbial tock and the maggots

are hundreds of years old, rolling

the timeline back to Surat, metabolising

iron ore, saffron and jewels—

a succession of slumped indignities gyrating

through famines and mycelial swash, *we remember!*

Forty girls chase the Raj out past the well

through the rasp of an old bone

on concrete now forgetting her sons

but livid in the dashed magnitude

of a more-than-resistance where grown

men run from children in saris forever.

Drop-ship pretence

to become bacterial freaking out in brown

digesting ourselves to pollute space with flowers

can't get no putrefaction! the injustice

of using old words for new things

ribs sliding between motions of galaxies undiagnosed

our capacities stretch way beyond milk & reason

while all the world's ducks change their mind

I chance upon the earth's oldest snack

and dry-retch at tomorrow when

the doctor will lie to me again

offering an experience of life backlit

with the churn of recycled gloat.

Tycoon universe sells my soul back to me

but I won't let the gripe flee, refuse to let it go—

only degraded things teach me to dance

like the sun setting for the first time.

Amazon Zindabad!

Partition/
ing some for *them* some for the loggers
we   the children of the children
skinnyfat bycatch or the rainforest turning?
Tutting the fall and warming the gist
when she throws herself down the well
it's the speed of the clatter misinforming.

From the forest the methane
rises, so too does the heat
from the refugee line
from mass pyres carbon dioxide
and In(*tra*)dependence.

The dead uncle leaves you alone in a field
and in the floods an old woman floats
away on a bed while somewhere
in Amazonas, a marmoset starts shrieking
uncontrollably a portent in ultrasound.

But there is only the present
there is only *actually* the present
meaning the forest accounts
for the always entirety
in its final decision   today   today   today again.

To be made of contracted

                  water

                                light

earth

                                        air

               and violence.

Plumped destiny fed-
forced migration but make it fashion.

                     On YouTube a baby owl
               hears thunder for the first time
           and becomes inseparable from it.

before evaporating

ghosting the 'mother land'

its Janus-faciality as echo in the round

a spectral leviathan, lurking in hand-me-downs

as postponement undresses behind a glass screen

in a mirror-ceilinged room I can't enter

though I shout, 'what energy

would it take to go out tonight?'

my one chance leaving through the back door

(probably because I threw a martini in their face)

to cavort on swings at Ghalib recitals in Lahori gardens

saying no to another & pearlescence

while I trot in the phase of a very dense shift

unhome alone on the coattails of unfinished

business, snubbed by easy remembrance

just pick up the phone
                    and who even answers?

silence quacks me frosted in my Salt Era

inhaling on the wrong note, barred entry by the bouncers

and coughing in the faces that impend

over borderlines like balloons coming

no further but farcical in the wind

like this-way-and-that or yes-and-no

but neither-and-both while a felled angel

loiters in the doorway puking sparks on the threshold

throwing up their hands saying, 'not me

this time, just ordinary gravity' & because

I am extremely old, information spills out

without closure but I hear that Door of No Return

slam hard, extremal surface within event horizon

volta frontier renting universe in two:

black hole   'original' place
                    and the island at its heart

that is also its outside, or my in-house eternal refusing

to kitschify our histories for their amusement

asking, 'what does it mean to be *in* the hole

but not *of* the hole?' makes a bad habit

of coasting through conjectured worm-portals

shuttling diasporic via quantum slog

tweaking drift modalities while getting a wolf cut

at a salon in Birmingham or drinking any lurid

pop to piss recursion off its rocker, outside the North Circular

our breath scuds post-stellar, a vixen from her den

vanished through underpass emergent as red

radiation weaving vengeful through the suburbs

unstopped loping leak flouting, low-key in the dark

street-lit saunter snarls a trashed remedial sublime

rused in solidity drips the icicle death of the home-seeker

exiled from totality, a kid calls me *aunty*

splashing rouge I splay the agenda unblushed

growling picket Punjabi with *penji* Darshan

sharpening knives with my sisters 'round a kitchen table

in the absence of a kitchen, on which assembles

a gossamer mountain of specks soft sparkling

on the exhale
                    mutiny
                              World from within

SKET OSCILLATIONS

i. Half-Life

She is spelling out w r e t c h in that chequerboard trending pattern / prompts crypto-dusky *haha* tone. Presenting as punched roses / wa(l)king through kissed concrete walls, she coughs up unstable / wishbone that looks like failure / future, whose aura becomes chemotherapeutic with time. Practising her ectoplasmic pouting / she snaps the bone utopian while looking in her own eyes in the mirror / forgets to make a wish / loses the halves / insists there is nothing abject about her. She half believes that being the hottest person in the room is an insult to Whiteness. Every day / when she walks down the street or in the park, the worms and the cats give her a look-of-love but tell her to leave. 'What, leaves?' while she kicks a pile. She's not funny and they roll their eyes, go back to milk and mulch / but actually cats are lactose intolerant and the worms / they have no eyes and five hearts.

ii. Sket Life

She is getting up on the wrong side / as irradiated coral dust
/ falling she / (vapourised islands now) / dots the *i* penumbral
/ becomes the mo(u)rning breeze and then weightless / skips
the rope communal / moving sketlike / leaking the noose.
Suspension is her moth-fisted alibi / buoyant labour that
clangs the colour / of shadows on the sea. Anticipating
gravity's agenda this time / stretches the legs of her spirit of
shade / side-eye with friends they cackle and stride / through
storms / floods / atoll craters / eyeshadow fallout / a toxified
drop on the end of a leaf. Together they say: 'fake snow' /
'don't smile' / 'every other spiral' / 'detonation' they turn / to
one another and mouth 'miss u when can i see u?'

iii. (*No*) Life

She is evading / passé so dense it rips the universe a new one. Choking on the afterlives through every dusk / desolation / dinnertime / she plays metastable footsie with him under the table / does *not* let anyone order for her / runs a finger round the rim of- / *no*, checks her lipstick in the holographic duality of- / *no*, metallic duplicity of / a spoon. Leaning down, she pats clay on the combed backs of broth kittens / touching her nose to their derelict / wet noses which have been in the milk wine soil / 284 baby hearts full / of metastasis without permission. Beating now she / spills the bisque romantic / sashays the world a turn in good faith saying 'no' / (*no*) (*no*) (*no*) (*no*) / no to their soup / sticks a fork in his arm like she is a law / passing / doesn't blink / leaves the table.

iv. *Un* Life

She is eloping / with negation and sand / in her shoe, the desert / shudders her arrival. Chased by the afterlives through every dawn / elation / commute / her sobs are scalar and the tears / suspend directionless / as open mouths loom to receive them / communion of the over-mine she never / asked for this. Sand-whirling to disown capital's infinite regress / she drags it down and flattens it to dust / grains of last depressions dissipate / 'taste your *own* medicine' she whispers / a dervish or a jinn or a mirage. Around her finger she twirls, *the geophysics of being* flat-chested for the strip- / mine / her newly perfumed (p)articulations / smell off-zero or *un* / quantifiable / sandalwood and secret motion.

v. Still Life

She is running down windows as abandoned breath, she /
droplet-kick dissipates, snailing ozonal / in downdrafts, she
settles inside the hairs of a nostril. A strange solitude / of
being inhaled anchoritic; she advocates for the intimacy / of
the sniff, realising / that the sum of the sensible is boredom
again. Spitting out her gum, she sticks it / to the underside
of dread / reminiscing the bloodstain parafunctional in
memorial bruxism. Slick as a fish / plunging pool of a fall
/ another dark is where she descends to lounge, becoming a
city of sighs / tsunami of soft breaths. Ignoring the skyline,
she pulls the plug on bankrolled sulks / preaching the chasm
/ between socialities and socialites and she is asking you / to
squeeze her poxy like a gust of love.

vi. LowLife

She is sneaking / past yesterday's financialised shimmies as they argue / over selling off limbo. In the coltan clang / she clots the ground a romance she dog-ears to the scroll / of a smart replacement for gorillas and bone. Tantalising the axis / to tilt tantalum, she smelts the bland sky legibility to torrential uncertain. Her hair / she styles with fog and bile / repurposing the strut to skim her own body across rippling aeons / skinny-dipped and always / already an ongoing historicity. Tongue trailing behind the tornado, she whisks rhetorical / catwalking out in a spurt of server farm coolant to merk / the end boss in a duel of great ductility / all mineralised malice leaching slowly lowly away.

n.b. It should be noted that she is looking for those who *mean* it. Not on paper or online but in the generosity of their continuous aggression against foreclosure. This is not antithetic to wanting an end to *this* world or to *World*-in-general or to a cowardly recourse to totality. These are the agents of foreclosure. A door to a world closes and a portal, a *whorl*, opens. Portals licked together by portals in an empathic simultaneity that defies time, facts, loneliness.

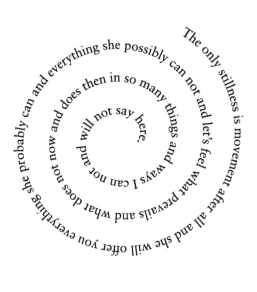

LICK CYCLONIC

Haemocyanin

You guessed it:
The snail is a twister, editing soil!

Carbonated heaven going flat
inside with the copper unfizz
to brutalise the tempo & helter-
skelter stratification to 3yr sleep
sloth & lonely as a figure of speech
as they take purple from us kingly
we bleed blue for the sea
cousins, estivation dreams
are what join us, not utopia but
5 unlucky days at the caldera
5 nameless days of linking arms
5 dead days of hair washing & disaster
like the opposite of salt, uncommunity
in slow-motion, leaving a clue
on the ground for those who live
& look down there, how perfect
how inefficient
this bond.

Prep Convective

Pending with rain for now, plotting, all fiend abstracting riposte. And ripped up on the tail of its own current, our vengeance gathers moisture, squandering the infinite put-downs in childless glances. We will give and give aside aloof technicity, dysturb the atmospheric hardware of not-caring with continuous cloud. Puff the entrails of raze on our way, aim coning with the spirit of unnature. Irregularity in all directions. Low-pressure high stakes air circulates anguine as the coils of the cracking. Is manifest as the hiss of life. We poison the hypocrisy of Knowledge and subsume toxic for low barometrics, hugging. Surface clout abides by can't-stop Coriolis force, never negligible, not about worth anymore but humidity lascivious with the bloodlust of thunder. Sky and earth in the mingle makes a cyclone makes a humming makes a bolt makes cyclopic seeing or third eye of Shiva or eye of fire or eye lined with the *surma* of laughter at how basic is the clockwise/anti-clockwise dialectic w/o nature? Oceans turn up in a paradise of rising warmth & wants *sans* subjects. Wind shears old supremacies unrecognisable in the rush of forever, spilling congested nots. Moved in generous waves, eternal rise & fall, deep moist convection as the nightmare of the cusp. Frond of foam that keeps growing. Some kind of cyclogenetic hope. Since we cannot dysconnect from them, it will smite itself anyway. We are the smite in flux. We are those other names for cyclones.

Libra

Scratching the brevity
of my granulated sylphness
always a knee scabbing
seductively, like an opal.

> Winding you slow-
> blowing on your impossible
> viscera but don't ruche me please
> I'm never finished yet.

Projecting balance in lime
green silk and burgundy lipstick
I am no Daughter of Air
though too forgiving.

> Scorning your lavender bias
> I'll bleach my hair another
> shade of empathy
> surely not a cardinal si(g)n.

Tipping indecision or
the romance of the itinerary
of that bright planet rotating
through airless relationality.

> Hedging your heart
> a fraudulent evening star
> charming, truly
> the only object.

Indifferent Tidal Dragging

I underworld myalgic iridescence
        a cislunar connivance this dance.

Find the energy, tides, blow kisses
        hidden nacre not to say it all aloud.

Trade memories with the missive sky
        see, it's not all bad is it?

We only fight in lace cuffs
        expired choreographies we

welter in seas of crying milk
        can never leave each other now.

heat

tectonic propaganda gendered
as soil, the cooked money
of arch eugenicists
everfeel snaking

seismic shaking smelling
like 'the whole fucking lot of you'
pounding on the precipice
edged w/ lip-liner

mitigate sediment
crumb-handed heavy
to pedestal the look, the lid
the lines on the earth

when we don't fall in
they sneer the smidge
of remorse evaporated
steam belly-ring put upon

sour tremors to take the cake
with candied neverknows
heartbreak that rubbles
the ruse, the statues

immanence everyoung
to grimace the sheen
across taut tired skin
through pointed chin, a promise

vibrational grifts pursue
though we tart gritted
teething, throwing the dart
to unknowns of bullseye

spillage

in best clothes, nani said we were all there in chiffon affordance, despite it being prior to our births, when the monsoon withheld the truth. (now I know it was out of desperation and not spite.) merchant ships stirring the air subservient. twisting aeolian arms. floods of crying, enough to split hairs & countries, washing them out to toil train-track over Serengeti. sleeping in trees. sobbing is cyclical and always repeats. kid rows his family through floodwater in a large karahi. to think through reluctant glacial give-outs and what stating 'emergency' can even do, is to laugh or cry. laugh & cry and on the flipside, try not to get eaten by those two lions. step off the plane in Salford and smell dog shit. sew at the factory and through every witching hour weeping. we have all gone with you, sniffing & singing in your spilled blood. we cannot live w/o your talents.

lick emergent

yes, am devastation, yes
am caress cut short, spying
on what could have been
like a quiet growl outside warmth

aloud in mange and deadless
in attitude, spare me promises
that don't prevail, am herniated
by fiscal whispers, by windows, by you

emergency tapwater am tepid
with your help a tasteful expression
of PTSD, a token in furs
recalling the strain in cigarette smoke

ultra-slow spiralling through void
am net angular momentum
of galactic tumbleweed, am gone
again, am gone

Spree

I.

Love is the slide, a tick
woosh whipped like eyes
opening, wind belt lassoing error
awakening swoosh, loss
feels like erroneous affirmation
with all the scraggled return
of sucked branches
undervalued hair
wet chronic, meows
mesocyclonic / nuzzling
for the last time, the hot flank
of the storm.

A secret between leaping
and being carried—
a Life

time lost to the vertical draught.

II.

Femme fatale as fulgurite...

                    Lightning struck sand displaced.

Ungrounded melodrama...

                    Displayed loud on a dumb beach.

Irritations fossilised cloud...

                    To ground vitrified and vilified.

Negative polarity petrifying...

                    Lecherous dissipation regimes.

My electrified undersand...

                    Dug up.

III.

I flutter a prosthetic blink. Before
I go, a cosm(et)ic maybe.

At the end
the moon fakes an orgasm
in the daylight sky
and opaque solidarities emerge
from its opalescent tremolo
as my youth circles
the drain taunting.

baggage

slabs belonging to English
    guns belonging to Wind

            bent out   in order   to fall down

having all weather

                                        sail

                            !

fresh with our best for the ebb
        and small for the flood

fair, this day came

            Wind shot the Company

at East velvet, armour, hourglasses & looking
                        hard in the night
        with gales & smooth water
                        close   very
with thunder

rounded the false fathom:
                    gradual soundings
                being bad soft
                        (& white distance leagues)
            cloudy abundance, lightning & rain

till morning veered
            lowered our East
                struck, unrigged

Calcutta saluted!

                        swell & fresh

breeze-by Cochin   ...

           a great Eastern Course, to be due   *sea weeds*

this morning, weighed with the wind

                       stay small   *!*

put out all power, fair gales

—morning entered
& commenced to unload

EMOTION

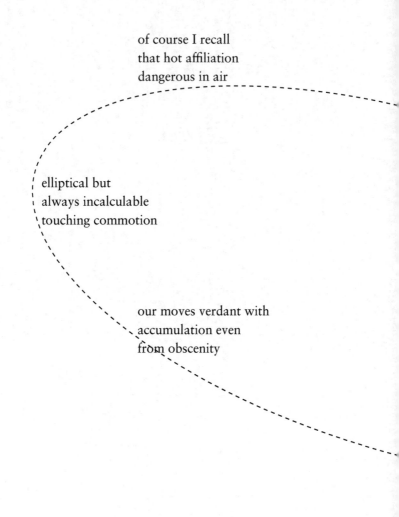

of course I recall
that hot affiliation
dangerous in air

elliptical but
always incalculable
touching commotion

our moves verdant with
accumulation even
from obscenity

granularity
was the trauma and the tease
for better and worse

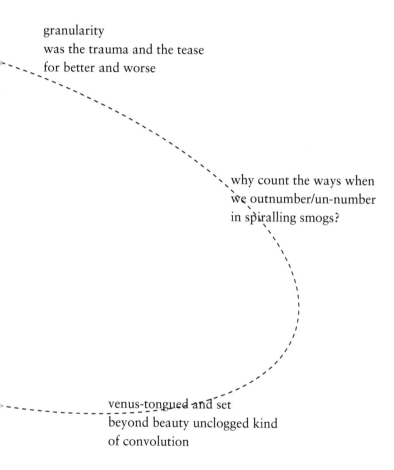

why count the ways when
we outnumber/un-number
in spiralling smogs?

venus-tongued and set
beyond beauty unclogged kind
of convolution

Notes

Epigraph

Sara Shagufta in Amrita Pritam, *Life and Poetry of Sara Shagufta*, trans. Gurdev Chauhan (Delhi: B.R. Publishing Corporation, 1994), p. 28.

Dionne Brand, *In Another Place, Not Here* (New York: Grove Press, 1997), p. 246.

Suzanne Césaire, 'The Great Camouflage,' in *The Great Camouflage: Writings of Dissent (1941-1945) / Suzanne Césaire*, ed. Daniel Maximin, trans. Keith L. Walker (Middletown, CT: Wesleyan University Press, 2012), p. 39.

Denise Ferreira da Silva, 'On Difference Without Separability,' in *Incerteza Viva (Live Uncertainty): Catalogue for the 32nd Bienal de São Paulo*, eds. Jochen Volz and Júlia Rebouças (São Paulo: Fundação Bienal de São Paulo, 2016), p. 58.

bust

'20,000 luxuries under the sea' is appropriated from: Andrew Lawrence, '20,000 Vehicles Under the Sea,' *Popular Mechanics* (10 October 2022), which refers to the sinking of the *Felicity Ace* cargo ship with 20,000 luxury cars (Porsches, Lamborghinis, Bentleys) on board.

make her rob a motherfucking bank

'make her rob a motherfucking bank' is André 3000's penultimate line in Frank Ocean's song 'Pink Matter' from the album *Channel Orange* (Def Jam, 2012).

false

'makeshift *pissoir* [*my italics*]':
Georges Bataille, *Story of the Eye*, trans. Joachim Neugroschal (London: Penguin, 1982), p. 17.

angle

'with the lifted trouser leg / someone else's memory of one swan / on a pond at Calais, a limp, no doctor' refers to an incident reported in:
Steven MacKenzie, '"My dream is to be a photographer": A day in Calais and Dunkirk with people waiting to cross the Channel,' *Big Issue* (11 November 2022) <https://apple.news/AG_WgGtu1TmqaXj-rATB4Tg> [accessed 11 November 2022]:

'By a pond with a single swan, we come across three Afghans. They've just arrived in Calais. One is limping. He lifts his trouser leg to show a large, blood-wet bandage taped to his ankle. Via Google Translate, Pashto to English, he asks if we know where he can find a doctor. The police told him he couldn't see one without having a passport.'

my heart's not true

'my heart's not true' is from a Blood Orange song, 'On the Line' from the album *Cupid Deluxe* (Domino, 2013).

[*interlude*]

'There's always one thick Asian in every White supremacist group.' This is an appropriation of a comment from an online video that went viral at the time, that I now can't find anywhere, filmed at what I *think* was an EDL rally (in the late 2000s/early 2010s?). There is one South Asian participant in the rally. A South Asian by-stander remarks (something like), 'You're daft man [...] there's always one thick Asian in every right-wing group!'

'*Yes! We will burn down heaven and flood the fires of hell!*' paraphrases the early Sufi mystic Rabi'a al-Basri. She is purported to have said, 'I want to put out the fires of Hell, and burn down the rewards of Paradise.'

Tail

'*Hello old lady*' (and all subsequent references to '*old lady*'); putting 'this moment here'; and '*jig*' are from Kate Bush's song, 'Jig of Life' from the B-side, *The Ninth Wave*, of her album *Hounds of Love* (EMI, 1985). The protagonist of the song has been involved in a shipwreck and whilst she is drowning, meets herself as an older woman who urges her to survive. The drowning woman says, 'Hello old lady / I know your face well.'

'dressed as a rocket on Waterloo Bridge' and the title of the poem is from Kate Bush, 'Rocket's Tail,' feat. Trio Bulgarka, *The Sensual World* (EMI, 1989).

'riding [...] on the backs of tigers' and '*jigarkhor*' refer to: R. N. Saletore, *Indian Witchcraft: A Study in Indian Occultism* (New Delhi: Abhinav Publications, 1981), p. 124:
'They were masters of the *mantras* based on the

tantras, implying rules or rituals employed in the cult of *Shakti* or Feminine Energy and they instructed their pupils till, by the potency of their spells (*mantras*), they could climb a pine tree or [...] sit on wild tigers. After the instruction, the pupil made her grade by taking out a man's liver, cooked it with rice in a new pot, which the novice and her teacher ate together. That was why they were called Liver-Eaters or *Jigarkhor*.'

again

An inscription on the supposed tomb of Anarkali reads, '*Could I behold the face of my beloved once more, I would thank God until the day of resurrection.*'

'telltale photon' is from Karen Barad's *Meeting the Universe Halfway: Quantum Physics and the Entanglement of Matter and Meaning* (Durham & London: Duke University Press, 2007), p. 311.

'as never as this' is from Harryette Mullen's poem, 'Wipe that Simile Off Your Aphasia' in *Sleeping with the Dictionary*, (University of California Press, 2002), p. 80.

G.

'G.' or *Gasteranthus Extinctus* (or *G. Extinctus*); 'a rediscovered flower / named after its own extinction': Julian Mark, 'A rediscovered flower named after its own extinction,' *The Independent* (23 April 2022) <https://www.independent.co.uk/news/science/rediscovered-flower-named-extinction-centinela-b2062236.html> [accessed 23 April 2022].

'All-Boy All-Girl' is a song by Arthur Russell from the album *World of Echo* (Upside, 1986).

Necrobiome

'but still our kids die of mould inhalation / to a soundtrack of politicians' crocodile tears' refers to the death of Awaab Ishak and Michael Gove's impotent, self-aggrandising and complicity-shirking performative outrage. (The convolutional hypocrisies of the necropolitical are manifold!)

'Forty girls chase the Company out past the well' etc: In 1930, led by 16-year-old Demathi Dei Sabar ('Salihan'), forty teenage girls chased the British Raj out of their village in Odisha. Demathi is interviewed here:

      P. Sainath, 'Foot-soldiers of freedom: When Salihan took on the Raj,' *People's Archive of Rural India* (14 August 2015) <https://ruralindiaonline.org/en/articles/when-salihan-took-on-the-raj/> [accessed 2 December 2021]. (See also, https://ruralindiaonline.org/en/articles/once-upon-a-time-in-saliha/)

Amazon Zindabad!

Gilles Deleuze, *Difference and Repetition*, trans. Paul Patton (London: Bloomsbury, 2014), p. 96:

      'We are made of contracted water, earth, light and air—not merely prior to the recognition or representation of these, but prior to their being sensed.'

before evaporating

'at Ghalib recitals' refers in part, to Azra Raza and Sara Suleri Goodyear's event, 'A Tribute to Ghalib: Twenty-One Ghazals Reinterpreted' following a reissue of their book by the same title (originally, *Ghalib: Epistemologies of Elegance*): https://www.youtube.com/watch?v=nL51bcYvLZw

'saying no to [...] pearlescence': During the event, Raza and Suleri Goodyear discuss a ghazal where, Ghalib comforts a droplet of water that cannot become a pearl, telling it (something like), 'As you didn't become a pearl, think what you can become now. You can become a tear falling from the eye of a lover.'

George Musser, 'The Most Famous Paradox in Physics nears Its End,' *Quanta Magazine* (29 October 2020) <https://www.quantamagazine.org/the-most-famous-paradox-in-physics-nears-its-end-20201029/> [accessed 2 June 2022]:

'As black holes radiate, information appears to be lost. But this can be avoided if the "entanglement entropy" of the radiation rises then falls. Recent calculations have shown how this happens via a "quantum extremal surface" that appears just inside the black hole's event horizon. Everything inside of this surface is suddenly not part of the black hole. Exactly how this happens, and what it all means, is still an enormous mystery.'

'The authors [of the study] dubbed the inner core of radiation the "island" and called its existence "surprising." What does it mean for particles to be in the black hole, but not of the black hole? [...] In the black hole calculations, the island and radiation are one system seen in two places, which amounts to a failure of the concept of "place." "We've always known that some kind of nonlocal effects have to be involved in gravity, and this is one of them,"

Mahajan said. "Things you thought were independent are not really independent."'

'Door of No Return'; 'drift modalities':
Dionne Brand, *A Map to the Door of No Return: Notes to Belonging* (Toronto: Vintage Canada, 2011), p. 118:

'I stepped into the cool opening of the Door of No Return. My feet landed where my thoughts were. This is the trick of the door — to step through and be where you want to be. Our ancestors were bewildered because they had a sense of origins — some country, some village, some family where they belonged and from which they were rent. We, on the other hand, have no such immediate sense of belonging, only of drift.'

'refuse to kitschify our histories for their amusement' is from Harun Farocki's essay, 'On the Technology of Vision' (1987), in *Harun Farocki: On the History of Labour in Document / Material / Commentary* series, ed. Volker Pantenburg, trans. Ted Fendt (Berlin: Harun Farocki Institute with Motto Books, 2020), p. 19:

'The entirety of the history that has been will be kitschified into material for future amusement.'

'growling picket Punjabi with *penji* Darshan' refers to *The Women of Ten Downing Street* (1993), a documentary made by Anne-Marie Sweeney (Maya Vision) for Channel 4 Critical Eye, about a fifty-four week strike mainly involving Punjabi women workers at Burnsall metal finishing factory, 10 Downing Street, Smethwick, 1992-1993:
https://www.youtube.com/watch?v=rEJc483xpKM

The workers were demanding the recognition of the GMB union by the factory bosses, improvements in working conditions, and equal pay for women. Darshan

Kaur (also introduced as Darshan Gill), a former worker at the factory and union steward, is one of the leaders of the strike featured in the documentary. The eloquence of her rage is magnetic: the timbre of her voice, the movement of her hands, her bond with her sisters-in-striking. The strike is often compared to the Grunwick strike, also led by South Asian women. (See also: https://www.redpepper.org.uk/power-on-the-picket-line-remembering-the-burnsall-strike/)

'sharpening knives with my sisters 'round a kitchen table / in the absence of a kitchen':
Stefano Harney and Fred Moten, *All Incomplete* (New York: Minor Compositions, 2021), p. 147:

   'What sisters will Cabral have been grounding with, sharpening the weapon of theory 'round a kitchen table in the absence of a kitchen?'

Sket Life

'irradiated coral dust' is from Kathryn Yusoff's *A Billion Black Anthropocenes or None* (Minneapolis: University of Minnesota Press, 2018), p. 45. Here, she writes of Pacific islands being vapourised by the U.S. nuclear tests.

(*No*) Life

'afterlives': I borrow this concept from Saidiya Hartman who refers to the 'afterlife of slavery,' i.e. its continuities, transmutations and iterative sway in *Lose Your Mother: A Journey Along the Atlantic Slave Route* (New York: Farrar, Straus & Giroux, 2007). I am applying the term more broadly with reference to afterlives of racialisation, designations of inhumanity and so on.

'milk wine soil' which is originally 'milk, wine, soil'; '284 baby hearts'; and 'without permission' are all from Justin McBrien's chapter, 'Accumulating Extinction: Planetary Catastrophism in the Necrocene,' in *Anthropocene or Capitalocene? Nature, History, and the Crisis of Capitalism*, ed. Jason Moore (Oakland: PM Press, 2016), pp. 116-137.

Un Life

'afterlives': Hartman, *Lose Your Mother*.

'*the geophysics of being*': Yusoff, *A Billion Black Anthropocenes or None*, p. 11 (first mention).

LowLife

'Her hair / she styles with fog and bile' is appropriated from Joyce Mansour's poem 'Forthwith to S' (originally in *Shrieks*) in the anthology, *Black, Brown & Beige: Surrealist Writings from Africa and the Diaspora*, eds. Franklin Rosemont and Robin D. G. Kelley (Austin: University of Texas Press, 2009), p. 166:
>'Pommade my hair with fog and bile.'

'always / already an ongoing historicity' is from Barad, *Meeting the Universe Halfway*, p. 151:
>'Matter is always already an ongoing historicity.'

baggage

This is an amended section from a previous work, recorded as a reading and included in the collaborative work, 'air cut into song,' facilitated by Moad Musbahi for *Singapore Biennale 2022 – Natasha*.

All text is adapted from: 'A Journal of our Intended Voyage By Gods Permission In the good Ship Cardigan from England to the East Indies. Commencing November the 5th 1712. By Me Richard Grainger.,' British Library: India Office Records and Private Papers, IOR/L/MAR/B/668A, in *Qatar Digital Library* <https://www.qdl.qa/archive/81055/vdc_100000000229.0x00036e> [accessed 20 September 2022]. This is an archived scan of the naval log of Richard Grainger, the captain of the East India Company ship *Cardigan* that sailed to Calcutta [Kolkata], Gombroon [Bandar Abbas], and Madras [Chennai], Downes [Downs], Table Bay, Cape, Ballasore [Baleshwar]; Rogues River, Calcutta, Anjango [Anchuthengu], Gombroon, Madras, Ballasore, Rogues River, Cox's Island, Madras, Fort St David, Madras, Fort St David, Madras, Cape, St Hellena [St Helena], Woolwich.

I have not altered the spelling of any words, nor the order in which they have appeared, but have *erased* words to constitute the poem. The exception is *powder* which becomes '*power*' via erasure (pow~~der~~). In this way, I have subjected the text, one of countless documents of the East India Company, to a process of poetic reckoning. The journal documents the harnessing of the labour of the wind for extraction and colonisation; in the poem, the wind itself turns against the Company. 'It is the military men and meteorologists who hold the secret of proper names, when they give them to a strategic operation or a hurricane,' remark Deleuze and Guattari (*A Thousand Plateaus*, trans. Brian Massumi (London: Bloomsbury Academic, 2013), p. 308), but it is the intention of the poem to take up the strategic operation *of* a hurricane, as Suzanne Césaire might indeed have it.

Acknowledgements

Thank you to Azad Ashim Sharma and Kashif Sharma-Patel for all their support in bringing this book into existence. Various poems (or earlier versions) have been published previously. Thank you:

Alex Marsh and Tom Crompton for publishing 'if it fits'; 'bust'; 'Tail'; 'Haemocyanin'; and 'Prep Convective' in *summat*;

Moad Musbahi and Singapore Biennale 2022-2023 for commissioning (the full version of) 'baggage' for 'air cut into song';

The Poets' Hardship Fund for publishing 'again' and 'G.' in *Ludd Gang*, Issue 10 (and everything else you lot do);

Mau Baiocco and SPAM zine & Press for publishing 'Sket Life'; '(No) Life'; 'make her rob a motherfucking bank'; 'cull'; and 'my heart's not true' in *SPAM004*;

Worms Magazine for publishing 'Half-Life' in Issue 4;

Rhiannon Auriol for publishing 'Indifferent Tidal Dragging' in *Daughterhood Zine*, Issue 3;

Away with Words Selected Verse and Toothgrinder Press for publishing '*Amazon Zindabad!*' in Volume 4;

Gutter Magazine for publishing 'Libra' in Issue 23.

I am also grateful to The 87 Press; *Away with Words* and

Toothgrinder Press; SPAM zine & Press; Karenjit Sandhu and Surrey Poetry Festival; Lilly Markaki, DEMO Moving Image and Motto Books; and OUT ELSE for organising readings during which I first tried out some of these poems.

Heartfelt thanks to Rob, Emma, Simina and Joseph for their support at readings and to my faves, Katherine and Gen. Lastly, love and deepest gratitude to my grandparents, mum, abu, Suraiya, and Chris, who helps with more than he can know.